THE SECRET THOUGHTS OF

CATS

THE SECRET THOUGHTS

OF

CATS

BY

CJ Rose

THE
collective
BOOK STUDIO

As you might
have suspected,
Mr. Goldfish,
I have terrible
news for you.

Excuse me, but I have a better idea. How about you chase the mice and I sit around all day watching Netflix.

Does this come in mouse flavor?

Hey, do you have that toy with the feather-thingy on it handy?

I bring sad tidings concerning the canary.

This generic kibble is not cutting it.

Oh, we are definitely smarter than the humans. I mean, do you go to a job you hate five days a week?

Can you change this please, but right after you get my dinner?

Call the fire
department!

Did she just say,
"No more cat treats"?

Who invited
that over?

"Bath time" stinks.

Now I simply
let dinner fly
right to me.

I realize that you have never seen anything quite as amazing as me before, but you will just have to get used to it.

For the last time,
I am not a
"kitty cat."
I am a petite tiger.

The human still looks
mad that I attacked
her leg.

How about you
pick *me* up instead of
this dusty old book?

No, it is *not* the wet food that is making me gain weight. It's the fact that I hardly ever move.

I certainly do not want to go on a trip with you. This is just super cozy.

I am pretty sure that
when this goes down,
I can pin it on the dog.

Well, hello handsome.

Clearly the whole "last one to the top of the branchless tree is a rotten egg" thing was a prank to get me stuck up here.

I guess that I need to wake up from this nap, so that I can get ready for bed.

Sorry, but I can recognize farmed salmon a mile away.

Was it you playing the loud music half the night?

Worship me as your ancestors did.

I know that it seems ridiculous, but if you pet me one more time I will attack you.

Look, human, your two favorite things in one place.

I love you, big orange ball in the sky.

No, I am serious.
If you poo in a box at
my house, a hairless
ape with a plastic
shovel will come and
take it away.

Oh, I love when they bring out the giant cat toy once a year.

It's pretty early in the morning . . . Probably time to go sleep on the human's face for a little while.

Has that tail-pulling kid left yet?

Change the channel already!

That's the spot!

What?
The dog ran away?
Best news ever!

That's it.
Put your back into it.

I resent that "old barn cat" remark.

Why can't he just be courteous and use his tongue to clean me?

I'm on the fence
about it. Literally.

I disagree with
the man-ape.
You look terrible
in those jeans.

Purrfect. Now please try not to move.

Let's both agree that today's was the last vet visit for awhile.

How about we keep the whole "me falling in the pool" story just between us?

That catnip stuff is great!

Certainly you don't think that I had anything to do with this?

Even though he does my every bidding, I am still growing weary of the human's foolish behavior.

Oh, I can still taste
that delicious mouse.

That's the last time
I stay up so late
yowling in the alley
with the guys.

No, I don't need your help getting down. Only if it would make you feel better.

I will never forgive you for taking the bird away from me.

I don't like the sound of the word "diet."

If the human isn't back with the milk soon, I think we should pee on his bed.

I will play with you, Mr. Ball, but only if you promise not to get stuck under the couch again.

Where is the handle
on this thing?

Oh, were these yours? Or are you here for one of the peppers?

Please excuse me, but I am about to make a spectacle of myself with this ball of yarn.

Agreed. We can be besties forever.

Library of Congress catalog in Publication data is available.

ISBN 978-1-951412-23-4
LCCN 2021931852

Printed and bound in China by
Reliance Printing Company Limited, Shenzhen

Cover and interior design by AJ Hansen.
All images courtesy of Shutterstock.

10 9 8 7 6 5 4 3 2 1

Published by The Collective Book Studio
4517 Park Blvd., Oakland, CA 94602